Poetic Word

Poetic Word

Ministering through Entertainment

WILLIAM CHAUKE

RESOURCE *Publications* • Eugene, Oregon

POETIC WORD
Ministering through Entertainment

Copyright © 2020 William Chauke. All rights reserved. Except for brief quotations in critical publications or reviews, no part of this book may be reproduced in any manner without prior written permission from the publisher. Write: Permissions, Wipf and Stock Publishers, 199 W. 8th Ave., Suite 3, Eugene, OR 97401.

Scripture quotations taken from The Holy Bible New International Version® NIV®
Copyright ©1973, 1978, 1984, 2011 by Biblica, Inc.™
Used by permission. All rights reserved worldwide.

Resource Publications
An Imprint of Wipf and Stock Publishers
199 W. 8th Ave., Suite 3
Eugene, OR 97401

www.wipfandstock.com

PAPERBACK ISBN: 978-1-7252-6281-2
HARDCOVER ISBN: 978-1-7252-6278-2
EBOOK ISBN: 978-1-7252-6279-9

Manufactured in the U.S.A. 02/03/20

Contents

Acknowledgements ix
Introduction xi

Part I: Sonnets

1. David — 2
2. Gospel of hope — 3
3. Jesus Christ — 4
4. Mentorship — 5
5. The Resurrection — 6

Part II: Free Verse

6. Adam and Jesus — 8
7. Being born again — 9
8. Changeless God — 10
9. Covenantal God — 11
10. God's grace — 12
11. God's Sovereign election — 13
12. Paul — 14
13. The First and the Last — 15

Part III: Limericks

14. Children of blessing — 18
15. Children of the light — 19
16. Contentment — 20
17. Godless chatter — 21

18. His precious blood	22
19. Real faith	23
20. Put your trust in God	24
21. Receiving from God	25
22. Reconciliation	26
23. Refining furnace of suffering	27
24. Reward for generosity	28
25. The diligent worker	29
26. The faithful witness	30
27. True prophecy	31
28. Walking by the Spirit	32

Part IV: Ballads

29. Discipline	34
30. Hezekiah	35
31. Higher glory	36
32. Omnipotent God	37
33. Omniscient God	38

Part V: Notes

Introduction	41
Note 1: David	41
Note 2: Gospel of hope	42
Note 3: Jesus Christ	43
Note 4: Mentorship	44
Note 5: The Resurrection	45
Note 6: Adam and Jesus	46
Note 7: Being born again	46
Note 8: Changeless God	47
Note 9: Covenantal God	47
Note 10: God's grace	48
Note 11: God's Sovereign election	49
Note 12: Paul	49
Note 13: The First and the Last	50
Note 14: Children of blessing	50
Note 15: Children of the light	51
Note 16: Contentment	52
Note 17: Godless Chatter	53
Note 18: His precious blood	53
Note 19: Real faith	54

Note 20: Put your trust in God	54
Note 21: Receiving from God	55
Note 22: Reconciliation	55
Note 23: Refining furnace of suffering	56
Note 24: Reward for generosity	56
Note 25: The diligent worker	57
Note 26: The faithful witness	57
Note 27: True prophecy	57
Note 28: Walking by the Spirit	58
Note 29: Discipline	59
Note 30: Hezekiah	59
Note 31: Higher glory	60
Note 32: Omnipotent God	61
Note 33: Omniscient God	62

Acknowledgements

First and foremost, I would like to thank our Lord and Savior, Jesus Christ, for his favor in calling me to the Teaching Ministry manifested through this book. I also want to thank the Lord Jesus for inspiring me through the Holy Spirit to write Christian poetry for his glory.

Second, I would like to extend my gratitude to my late father, for having brought me up in a Christian home. May his dear soul rest in eternal peace!

Next, I also want to thank all the pastors and men of God—too numerous to mention by name—who nurtured me in the Christian walk.

Last, and by no means least, I want to thank my dear wife Grace for bearing with me as I burnt the 'midnight oil' in the writing of this book.

Introduction

The title of this book, "Poetic Word: Ministering through Entertainment," implies that the book is based on the word of God and uses poetry as an entertaining medium for ministering. This gives rise to the concept I am labelling "ministainment": a combination of the first letters of the word "ministering" and the last letters of the word "entertainment"; whereby entertainment is in the foreground, while biblical instruction is in the background.

As the youth enjoy being entertained, this book of Christian poetry is primarily meant for them, as a resource for bible study, and peer-to-peer witnessing.

The secondary audience for the book comprises pastors, youth leaders, and teachers who may use the poems as the basis for imparting diverse Christian themes and values to their respective audiences during bible study sessions.

Last, but not least, the book is designed for all poetry enthusiasts who will become intensely exposed to biblical themes and values, as they enjoy and critique specific poetic formats contained in this book. As the reader peruses through the poems, they are likely to acquire biblical knowledge and critical Christian values for their own spiritual growth.

The author of this book was inspired by the Holy Spirit during the compilation process. During the compilation of the first five or so poems, the author would be led by the Holy Spirit to recite some poetic lines during

Introduction

prayer and meditation. Afterwards, he would be led to finalize the same poems.

During the next phase of revelation, the author would be given a specific theme or value; be led by the Holy Spirit to relevant scriptural texts, before being urged to compile poems on the same. Alternatively, while reading the word of God, the author would be urged by the Holy Spirit to write a poem on the subject matter of the biblical passage on hand. Notwithstanding that, the Holy Spirit allowed the author to choose the four poetic genres to work with.

The above-mentioned revelatory process continued until thirty three poems were compiled. Incidentally, thirty three is the age at which our Lord and Savior, Jesus Christ, was crucified for our redemption at Calvary. The poems, therefore, point to and are about Jesus, and his redemption of the world.

The compilation of this book is a clear demonstration of the fact that the word of God is active and alive, as well as liveable, since its author received revelation from the Holy Spirit, through words of knowledge—one of the diverse spiritual gifts. See the scriptural reference cited below for your encouragement:

> "To one there is given through the Spirit a message of wisdom,
> to another a message of knowledge by means of the same Spirit."
> —1 Corinthians 12:8 NIV

While the purpose of this book is to provide a resource and medium for bible study and witnessing, it is also intended to whet readers' appetites to embrace poetry as a powerful artistic form of expression in its own right.

This book is divided into five parts as follows:

1. Part I: Sonnets.
2. Part II: Free verse.
3. Part III: Limericks.
4. Part IV: Ballads.
5. Part V: Notes.

To guard against the usual pitfalls of having the instructional value of the poems being lost in the teeming forest of entertainment, the author suggests that the poems be used as the basis for more substantive bible study on diverse biblical themes.

Introduction

While the author provides some Scriptures in the Notes section of this book, they are not exhaustive but simply serve to provide a foundation for more exhaustive bible study. The reader is therefore encouraged to consult as widely as possible the relevant scriptural texts for their own spiritual growth.

As you go through this book, I pray that you be filled with the Holy Spirit and receive some of the spiritual gifts he may choose to give you in order to make you more effective in your given ministry.

PART I

Sonnets

1. DAVID

God's anointing
Follows heart's condition,
To man's confounding;
Who looks at outward condition.

Outwardly his brothers looked impressive,
And Samuel thought Eliab would be anointed,
Since David never looked impressive;
 But God would have none of the brothers anointed.

Inexperienced in the ways of war
Was David the shepherd boy;
Yet by a slingshot he slew Goliath in war,
Making all Israel verily coy.

Women then sang, "Saul has slain his thousands;
 And David his tens of thousands."

2. GOSPEL OF HOPE

Driving away the darkness;
Is the gospel of hope,
That pierces through the darkness,
With the rays of welcome hope.

It brings life to a lifeless world;
Freedom to the spiritually fettered,
Reconciliation to a polarized world,
And relief to the physically fettered.

It ministers to the whole person;
And embraces the whole church,
Catering to body soul and spirit-the whole person,
 And includes orphans and widows-the whole church.

It's a refuge for the spiritually and emotionally oppressed,
And a shelter to the physically oppressed.

3. JESUS CHRIST

Though being the Most High;
You became lowly man,
So we would know the Most High,
Who had become like man.

Though you were of Highest Royalty;
You clothed yourself in lowly humanity,
And Forsake you did your lofty Royalty,
So you would save lowly humanity.

Though blameless you became sin;
To become the perfect example of humility,
In order to purge us of all sin,
Thereby displaying your great humility.

You chose death on the cross though being God,
That we might live forever with you as our God.

4. MENTORSHIP

A perfect example was Jesus to mentorship,
He mentored his disciples-the followers.
Today church leaders from Jesus have mentorship,
So they may mentor their own followers.

Jesus taught practised and had disciples practise,
Giving his followers a perfect example.
Good mentors teach practise and have followers practise,
Giving them also a good model example.

Jesus as a good model did as he said,
To show the world the model behaviour.
Today models should do as they would have said,
To show followers model behaviour.

Mentors did freely receive,
So freely their followers should receive.

5. THE RESURRECTION

Through a man just one man
Did the curse of death come
And through a man just one man
Did the blessing of resurrection also come

And as is decreed that a grain must die
To yield a crop more glorious and fruitful
So to sin man must also die
To yield at the resurrection a body more glorious and fruitful

At death is sown a body
That by nature is mortal
Yet the resurrection yields a body
That is in nature immortal

Jesus is the resurrection and the life
And he will raise all who believe to eternal life

PART II

Free Verse

6. ADAM AND JESUS

An imperfect pattern of the one to come
Was Adam
And the perfect one who did come
Was Jesus

The only 'son' of God on earth
Was Adam
And the only Son of God in heaven
Was Jesus

The first man
Was of the dust of the earth
But the second man
Was of heaven

One disobedient act by Adam
Condemned mankind
Yet one obedient act by Jesus
Justified mankind

One sinful act by Adam
Made all sinners
But one righteous act by Jesus
Made all righteous

Death came through a man
Through Adam we all die
But life came through a man
Through Jesus we all live

Impacting humanity negatively
Was the first Adam
Yet impacting humanity positively
Was the second Adam

7. BEING BORN AGAIN

Of church sacraments one is water baptism,
Being a symbol of being born again,
Into God's family of holiness;
Achieved in reality through spiritual baptism.

Comes the Holy Spirit at water baptism,
Regenerating a spirit degenerate,
Making believers truly born again,
By spiritual baptism.

In baptism believers are submerged,
Dying to sin with Christ,
And in baptism believers emerge,
To a new life with Christ.

8. CHANGELESS GOD

Changeless you remain,
From eternity past
To eternity in the future;
Oh changeless God!

I, the Lord changes not
You say in your word;
For the same you remain yesterday today and tomorrow,
Oh changeless God!

Changeless you remain,
And faithful you remain
Though faithless man becomes,
Oh changeless God!

Changeless you remain,
And truthful you remain
While truth-less man becomes,
Oh changeless God!

I, the Lord changes not like shifting shadows,
You say in your word;
For your spiritual gifts and call irrevocably remain,
Oh changeless God!

9. COVENANTAL GOD

As a covenantal God,
Covenants old and new
You did provide to mankind,
As our covenantal God.

Two covenants you did provide;
The old being succeeded by the new,
As the old became obsolete,
For you are a covenantal God.

The old covenant you engraved on stone,
A shadow of the more superior new,
Engraved on the hearts of man,
As a covenantal God.

Came the old covenant,
A shadow of the new
Being Jesus' atonement at Calvary,
Purposed by our covenantal God.

Ineffective was the old covenant,
But effective to save was the new,
Provided for in eternity past,
Only by our covenantal God.

10. GOD'S GRACE

Through Moses was given the law:
Through Jesus Christ came grace.
Not by works but by grace
Have we been saved.

A free gift of God is grace,
Received only through faith
In Christ's atonement,
So no man should boast.

Though the giver of life,
Our Lord suffered death,
Demonstrating unparalleled love,
So we also may enjoy eternal life.

11. GOD'S SOVEREIGN ELECTION

Those to inherit your kingdom,
You have chosen by Sovereign election,
Since only they are partakers of the kingdom,
A favor bequeathed only by your Sovereign election.

Of Rebekah's twins Jacob you chose,
And his older brother Esau you rejected,
Before they had done right or wrong,
Demonstrating your Sovereign election.

Of kings you raise up one,
And another bring down,
Without regard to any qualifications;
So immutable is your Sovereign election.

David a young shepherd boy became king,
Ahead of his brothers outwardly more impressive;
While Moses a murderer became a deliverer,
Only by your Sovereign election.

And regarding God's calling,
Saul a church destroyer,
Became Paul a church builder,
Only by your Sovereign election.

Some you made apostles and prophets,
While some pastors, evangelists and teachers,
With no regard to any works done,
But only by your Sovereign election.

12. PAUL

Degenerate souls
You do regenerate,
Through the 'washing of rebirth'
As of Paul, your faithful servant.

Saul the church persecutor
You did change to Paul the church promoter,
Showing your abundant grace
For Paul, your faithful servant.

Having decreed salvation for Gentiles,
The Damascene encounter you did use,
Transforming Saul
To Paul, your faithful servant.

Paul you did raise,
Ordaining him minister to the Gentiles,
And rolling out the gospel to all the world,
For Paul, became your faithful servant.

13. THE FIRST AND THE LAST

Lord you are the First and Last,
Without end of days you are the Last;
But having been before all creation you are the First,
And without beginning of days you are indeed the First.

First you did come in the resurrection,
As your elect will also come to the resurrection;
But of judgement your word will come last,
For no one speaks after the Last.

PART III

Limericks

14. CHILDREN OF BLESSING

    Having been called to be children of blessing,
    Repay not evil with evil but with blessing;
    Unlike those living in this dark world,
    Who believe an eye for an eye is the way of the world;
     Yet children of blessing also inherit a blessing.

15. CHILDREN OF THE LIGHT

>Our God is love and the Father of light,
>And those who love children of light;
>Yet haters are children of darkness,
>Because hatred is the fruit of darkness;
>But anyone loving brother or sister lives in the light.

16. CONTENTMENT

I have learned to always live in contentment,
Well-fed or hungry, with or without I live in contentment;
And enduring each and every situation,
I remain content in all manner of situation,
Because through Christ I always live in contentment.

17. GODLESS CHATTER

    Our calling is nonconformity to patterns of this world,
    But godless chatter is conformity to this world;
    That draws one into being ungodly,
    And joining the ranks of the ungodly;
    So conform not to the pattern of this world.

18. HIS PRECIOUS BLOOD

> In humility he became flesh and blood,
> Empathizing with those of flesh and blood;
> He died to break the power of death,
> And freed us from the fear of death,
> Once we were washed by his precious blood.

19. REAL FAITH

Believing what God would have said is faith,
But absence of corresponding action stifles that faith;
Rendering it impotent and without fruit,
Yet combining faith with deeds produces the required fruit;
As Abraham when called to a land he knew not of went in faith.

20. PUT YOUR TRUST IN GOD

>In chariots and horses do no put your trust,
>But in the God of all flesh do put your trust,
>Because nothing is too hard for him,
>Since all things were created by him;
>So in him should you put your trust.

21. RECEIVING FROM GOD

> We receive not because we do not ask,
> And with wrong motives we receive not when we ask;
> So ask that to others you may be a blessing,
> Since Christians should to others be a blessing;
> Being a channel of God's blessing when they ask.

22. RECONCILIATION

Through Jesus Christ God did make reconciliation,
Entrusting us with the ministry of reconciliation;
But the ungodly are given to hatred and conflict,
For to them the way of the world is conflict;
Yet God committed to his elect the message of reconciliation.

23. REFINING FURNACE OF SUFFERING

Exalted we are through our suffering,
Since perseverance comes out of suffering;
Just as perseverance moulds a good character,
A long-suffering and hopeful character,
Refined in the furnace of suffering.

24. REWARD FOR GENEROSITY

Wisdom calls one to sow generously,
As the wise also reap generously;
Unlike the foolish who sow sparingly,
And also reap sparingly;
But God also meets the needs of the wise generously.

25. THE DILIGENT WORKER

In everything you do be diligent as if working for the Lord,
For you serve not men but the Lord;
And as a Christian worker you are the light of the world,
Dispelling darkness from the entire world,
So as to receive your due reward from the Lord.

26. THE FAITHFUL WITNESS

He became man to show the power of experience,
And man's trials and temptations he had to experience;
That through experience he became a faithful witness,
Of man's frailties before God and became a true witness;
Owing to that which he did on earth experience.

27. TRUE PROPHECY

>Strive for the gift of prophecy,
>As the church is edified by true prophecy;
>Neglecting not to test every spirit,
>Since not from God comes every spirit;
>But truthful and consistent with sound doctrine is true prophecy.

28. WALKING BY THE SPIRIT

    Living to please God is walking by the Spirit,
    Not yielding to desires of the flesh but of the Spirit;
    As the Spirit coexists not with the flesh,
    But impurity, idolatry and drunkenness belong to the flesh;
    While pleasing God is to crucify the flesh and yield to the Spirit.

PART IV

Ballads

29. DISCIPLINE

Rebuking and disciplining those you love,
Like any loving father;
For to the elect you mete out punishment,
As their loving Father.

Punishing disobedience with failure,
You draw to yourself the elect,
As would any loving father:
For you're the loving Father of the elect.

Unpleasant may seem discipline,
But the elect will appreciate in eternity,
As like purest gold they shine
Purged of all dross, in eternity.

30. HEZEKIAH

In Jerusalem, was Hezekiah king of Judah who fell ill,
And being at the point of death,
When Isaiah visited with a message from the LORD,
Saying he surely would not escape from death.

Hezekiah bitterly wept, asking the LORD
To check his record, of walking before him faithfully.
And the LORD was so moved by Hezekiah's prayer,
That to Hezekiah was added fifteen years, for walking before him faithfully.

31. HIGHER GLORY

A grain of sand on the shore of eternity,
Is our temporary suffering,
As God draws us to himself,
Through present suffering.

In the noise of comfort, often we fail
To hear God's silent voice;
For in the silence of suffering is heard
More clearly God's silent voice.

In the cold and emptiness of suffering,
God says: "Come my child,"
For in the noise of opulence, often we fail
To hear God saying: "Come my child."

Drawing us from the comfort zone,
Suffering begets for us higher glory;
As we listen to God's calling:
A calling to higher glory.

32. OMNIPOTENT GOD

Is anything too hard for me, you declare
As an omnipotent God.
Can anyone save from my hand, you also declare
Only as an omnipotent God.

Can anyone open the door I've closed, you declare
As an omnipotent God.
Can anyone close the door I've opened, you also declare
Only as an omnipotent God.

33. OMNISCIENT GOD

Declaring the end from the beginning,
Is our omniscient God,
Who also gives prophesies of things not yet come,
As indeed an omniscient God.

Through prophets of old did you declare salvation's plan
In advance, as an omniscient God;
Who also did declare Satan's doom in advance,
As indeed an omniscient God.

Through prophets did you declare Jesus' virgin birth,
Only as does an omniscient God;
Who also to Adam did promise salvation's plan,
As indeed an omniscient God.

Oh, omniscient God
Do you declare things not yet come;
As in your fore-knowledge,
Things will be that are not yet come.

PART V

Notes

INTRODUCTION

In this book section, I will be taking the reader through some of the Scriptures relating to the different poems, while also throwing in a comment or two here and there, without necessarily being exhaustive. The reader is therefore encouraged to read more widely in order to appreciate more fully the themes, values, and virtues underpinning the cited poems.

NOTE 1: DAVID

The anointing of David to be king over his outwardly more impressive brothers, is a clear demonstration that God is not impressed by outward appearance but condition of the heart, which he knows full well as an omniscient God. See the Scripture below for further instruction on this subject:

> "But the LORD said to Samuel, "Do not consider his appearance or his height, for I have rejected him. The LORD does not look at the things people look at. People look at the outside appearance, but the LORD looks at the heart."
> —1 Samuel 16:7 NIV

The lesson to be learnt here is that Christians should strive to keep their hearts pure and free from sin, rather than putting on appearances of false piety.

God also knew the condition of David's heart: a heart of great faith and zeal for righteousness that enabled him to do great exploits. It was David's great faith, combined with his zeal for righteousness that energized him into appropriate action; resulting in the death of the lion, the bear, and giant Goliath. See the Scripture below for your appreciation of David's zeal for righteousness:

> "Your servant has killed both the lion and the bear; this uncircumcised Philistine will be like one of them, because he has defied the armies of the living God."
> —1 Samuel 17:36 NIV

David's statement of faith cited below also shows his total trust in God's protection:

> "David said to the Philistine, "You come against me with sword and spear and javelin, but I come against you in the name of the LORD Almighty, the God of the armies of Israel, whom you have defied . . . All those gathered here will know that it is not by sword or spear that the LORD saves; for the battle is the LORD's, and he will give all of you into our hands." "
> —1 Samuel 17:45; 47 NIV

NOTE 2: GOSPEL OF HOPE

"Gospel of hope" is a poem that encourages Christians to preach and live out a gospel with hope: a gospel that makes a real difference in people's lives, and holds the hope for eternal life. It espouses holiness and righteousness, and preaches a gospel of love and reconciliation, while ministering to the total person-body, soul, and spirit.

Christians are encouraged to reach out to the lost with the message of reconciliation as this gives the world the hope of eternal life. See the Scripture cited below for further details:

> "All this is from God, who reconciled us to himself through Christ and gave us the ministry of reconciliation: that God was reconciling the world to himself in Christ not counting people's sins against them. And he has committed to us the message of reconciliation."
> —2 Corinthians 5:18–19 NIV

A gospel of hope that is worth its salt promotes righteousness, and ministers to the needs of the total person. See the Scriptures below for further encouragement:

> "If we claim to have fellowship with him and yet walk in the darkness, we lie and do not live out the truth. But if we live in the light,

we have fellowship with one another and the blood of Jesus, his Son, purifies us from all sin."
—1 John 1:6–7 NIV

"Religion which God our Father accepts is this: to look after orphans and widows in their distress and to keep one from being polluted by this world."
—James 1:27 NIV

"He upholds the cause of the oppressed and gives food to the hungry. The LORD sets the prisoners free."
—Psalm 146:7 NIV

"The LORD is a refuge for the oppressed, a stronghold in time of trouble."
—Psalm 9:9 NIV

NOTE 3: JESUS CHRIST

This poem is an exhortation to Christians to be truly 'Christ-like,' by embracing Christ's virtues of humility and obedience, and of love and selflessness. See the Scripture below on Christ's humility and obedience:

"In your relationship with one another, have the same mindset as Christ Jesus: Who; being in very nature God, did not consider equality with God something to be used to his advantage; rather he made himself nothing by taking the very nature of a servant, being made in human likeness. And being found in appearance as a man, he humbled himself by becoming obedient to death-even death on a cross."
—Philippians 5:5–8 NIV

Jesus Christ demonstrated his great love and selflessness by leaving his position of comfort, power, and authority to come and die for our sins; so that we might live. See the Scriptures below for further details:

"For you know the grace of our Lord Jesus Christ, that though he was rich, yet for your sake, he became poor, so that you through his poverty might become rich."
—2 Corinthians 8:9 NIV

"For Christ also suffered once for sins, the righteous for the unrighteous, to bring you to God."
—1 Peter 3:18a NIV

NOTE 4: MENTORSHIP

The poem, "mentorship," is an exhortation to church leaders to emulate the example of our Lord and Savior Jesus Christ, regarding good mentorship. They should provide leadership development opportunities for their followers to grow in the direction of their gifting.

The Scripture cited below is a metaphor for mentorship or Christian discipling:

"As iron sharpens iron, so one person sharpens another."
—Proverbs 27:17 NIV

Jesus Christ, as the perfect mentor, taught his disciples; demonstrated or modelled appropriate behaviour, and then asked the latter to practice the required behaviour.

Jesus raised the dead; healed the sick, cast out demons, and exhorted multitudes to come to repentance. And when Jesus Christ sent out the twelve, he aptly gave them this instruction:

"As you go, proclaim this message: 'The kingdom of God has come near.' Heal the sick, raise the dead, cleanse those who have leprosy, drive out demons. Freely you have received; freely give."
—Matthew 10:7–8 NIV

As the perfect teacher and mentor, Jesus also used teachable moments to impart important values such as being prayerful. When the disciples failed to deliver a boy who had an epileptic spirit, Jesus underlined the significance of a prayerful life as shown in the dialogue cited below:

"After Jesus had gone indoors, his disciples asked him privately, "Why couldn't we drive it out?" He replied, "This kind can come out only by prayer.""
—Mark 9:28–29 NIV

Indeed, Jesus lived a very prayerful life, as shown in the following Scripture:

"But Jesus often withdrew to lonely places and prayed."
—Luke 5:16 NIV

NOTE 5: THE RESURRECTION

This poem provides a reassuring word to Christians, that though death came into the world through Adam's sin, all hope is not lost since Jesus Christ-the firstborn of the resurrection-overcame death, and will also raise those who die in him to eternal life. See the Scripture below for your enlightenment:

> "For since death came through a man, the resurrection of the dead comes also through a man. For as in Adam we all die, also in Christ all will be made alive."
> —1 Corinthians 15:21–22 NIV

The poem also shows us that what is sown must die in order to yield a crop more glorious and more fruitful, implying that to sin man must die, in order to yield at the resurrection, a body more glorious, and more rewarding. See the Scriptures below for further details:

> "How foolish! What you sow does not come to life unless it dies. When you sow you do not plant the body that will be, but just a seed, perhaps of wheat or something else. God gives it a body as he has determined, and to each kind of seed he gives its own body."
> —1 Corinthians 15:36–38 NIV

> "So it will be with the resurrection of the dead. The body that is sown is perishable: it is raised imperishable; it is sown in weakness, it is raised in power: it is sown a natural body, it is raised a spiritual body. If there is a natural body, there is also a spiritual body."
> —1 Corinthians 15:42–44 NIV

The poem also shows us that at the resurrection, Jesus will raise all who believe to eternal life and the unrighteous to eternal condemnation. See the Scriptures below for further details:

> "Jesus said to her, "I am the resurrection and the life. The one who believes in me will live, even though they die; and whoever lives by believing in me will never die. Do you believe this?" "
> —John 11:25–26 NIV

> "Do not be amazed at this for a time is coming, when all who are in their graves will hear his voice and come out-those who have done what is good will rise to live, and those who have done what is evil will rise to be condemned."
> —John 5:28–29 NIV

NOTE 6: ADAM AND JESUS

"Adam and Jesus" is a poem that uses the literary device of contrast to distinguish between Adam and Jesus; the earthly and the divine, man and God. Adam is presented as an imperfect picture of Jesus, because even though he does affect humanity, his influence is in the negative direction.

The attributes and influences of Adam and Jesus on humanity are reflected in the Scriptures cited below:

> "The first man was of the dust of the earth; the second man is of heaven."
> —1 Corinthians 15:47 NIV

> "Consequently, just as one trespass resulted in condemnation for all people, so also one righteous act resulted in justification and life for all people. For just as through the disobedience of one man the many were made sinners, so also through the obedience of the one man the many will be made righteous."
> —Romans 5:18–19 NIV

NOTE 7: BEING BORN AGAIN

Baptism is an important sacrament of the Christian faith, symbolizing death to sin and resurrection to a life of righteousness and holiness. It is this radical transformation in an individual's life, brought about by the sanctifying power of the Holy Spirit that is being referred to as being born again. Please note that water is used as a symbol of the Holy Spirit, hence "the washing of rebirth and renewal." Below, find the relevant scriptural references:

> "We were therefore buried with him through baptism into death in order that, just as Christ was raised from the dead through the glory of the Father, we too may live a new life."
> —Romans 6:4 NIV

> "He saved us through the washing of rebirth and renewal by the Holy Spirit."
> —Titus 3:5b NIV

NOTE 8: CHANGELESS GOD

Since God does not change, he is faithful and dependable. If God has promised you a particular ministry; hold fast to it, it will surely come to pass in the fullness of time because God does not operate in 'after-thought' mode since everything has been decreed in eternity past, as God revealed to Jeremiah that he had appointed him as a prophet before he was formed in his mother's womb (Jeremiah 1:5). In the meantime, strive for righteousness and holiness. See the Scriptures below for further encouragement:

> "I, the LORD do not change."
> —Malachi 3:6a NIV

> "Every good and perfect gift is from above, coming down from the Father of the heavenly lights, who does not change like shifting shadows."
> —James 1:17 NIV

> "Jesus Christ is the same yesterday and today and tomorrow."
> —Hebrews 13:8 NIV

> "For God's gifts and his call are irrevocable."
> —Romans 11:29 NIV

NOTE 9: COVENANTAL GOD

The above-mentioned poem refers to two covenants: the covenant of the law and the covenant of grace. The former was ineffective and served only as a shadow of the latter. The first covenant was ineffective because it was performed by sinful priests and through the offering of the blood of imperfect goats and calves. Nothing in nature is perfect! This explains why these sacrifices were offered continually.

Since God is holy and perfect, he could never be pleased by an imperfect sacrifice, hence the coming of our Lord and Savior Jesus Christ who became the ultimate sacrifice and atoned for our sins once and for all at Calvary, so that all who believe in him may be saved. See the Scriptures below for further enlightenment:

> "Day after day every priest stands and performs his religious duties; again and again he offers the same sacrifices, which can never

take away sins. But when this priest had offered for all time one sacrifice for sins, he sat at the right hand of God."
    —Hebrews 10:11–12 NIV

"The former regulation is set aside because it was weak and useless (for the law made nothing perfect), and a better hope is introduced, by which we draw close to God."
    —Hebrews 7:18–19 NIV

"For this reason Christ is the mediator of a new covenant, that those who are called may receive the promised eternal inheritance-now that he has died as a ransom to set them free from sins committed under the first covenant."
    —Hebrews 9:15 NIV

NOTE 10: GOD'S GRACE

This poem shows that the law-which could not save mankind was given through Moses, but grace came through Jesus, so that by believing in his atoning work at Calvary, mankind might be saved. It shows us that grace is a free gift from God and does not emanate from any good works we have done, so no man should boast. The poem also shows Jesus' unparalleled love and humility in that though he was God, he endured death on the cross for our sake. See the Scriptures below for your enlightenment:

"For the law was given through Moses; grace and truth came through Jesus Christ."
    —John 1:17 NIV

"He has saved us and called us to a holy life-not because of anything we have done but because of his own purpose and grace. This grace was given us in Christ Jesus before the beginning of time."
    —2 Timothy 1:9 NIV

"For it is by grace you have been saved through faith-and this is not from yourselves. It is the gift of God-not by works, so that no one can boast."
    —Galatians 2:8–9 NIV

NOTES

> "For you know the grace of our Lord Jesus Christ, that though he was rich, yet for your sake he became poor, so that you through his poverty might become rich."
> —2 Corinthians 8–9 NIV

NOTE 11: GOD'S SOVEREIGN ELECTION

This poem is a reminder to Christians that it is only God who decides on different callings and gifts in the church, in order to make them content with what they have and not become envious of other people's ministrations. See the Scriptures below for further encouragement:

> "But to each one of us grace has been given as Christ apportioned it."
> -Ephesians 4:7 NIV

> "Not only that, but Rebekah's children were conceived at the same time by our father Isaac. Yet before the twins were born or had done anything good or bad- in order that God's purpose in election might stand: not by works but by him who calls-she was told, "The older will serve the younger" . . . It does not, therefore, depend on human desire or effort, but on his mercy."
> —Romans 9:10–12; 16 NIV

NOTE 12: PAUL

The poem on Paul shows what it means to be truly born again. Paul was born again when Ananias prayed for him for the restoration of his sight and when he received the Holy Spirit. Evidence of his regeneration is borne by his radical change from being a church destroyer to a church builder and from being a church persecutor to a church promoter. See the Scripture below on Paul's regeneration:

> "Then Ananias went to the house and entered it. Placing his hands on Saul he said, "Brother Saul, the Lord-Jesus who appeared to you on the road as you were coming here-has sent me so that you may see again and be filled with the Holy Spirit.""
> —Acts 9:17 NIV

This poem also shows us that believers have diverse callings that God makes known to them. Paul was called primarily to preach the gospel to the

Gentiles, that is, the rest of the world beside Israel. Indeed Paul remained faithful to his calling as he has been credited with being the greatest missionary of his time and for writing most of the New Testament-a medium for the preaching of the gospel of Jesus Christ to the entire world. See Paul's own confession of his calling cited below:

> "He gave me the priestly duty to proclaim the gospel of God, so that the Gentiles might become an offering acceptable to God, sanctified by the Holy Spirit."
> —Romans 15:16b NIV

The story of Paul serves as a shining example to all believers to faithfully embrace their diverse callings.

NOTE 13: THE FIRST AND THE LAST

While the title "The First and the Last" also refers to God the Father and the Holy Spirit, the two Scriptures cited below contextually refer to Jesus Christ":

> "When I saw him, I fell at his feet though dead. Then he placed his right hand on me and said, "Do not be afraid. I am the First and the Last. I am the Living One; I was dead, and now look, I am alive forever and ever! And I hold the keys of death and Hades." "
> —**Revelation 1:17–18 NIV**

> "To the angel of the church in Smyrna write: These are the words of him who is the First and the Last, who died and came to life again."
> —Revelation 2:8 NIV

Revelation 1:17–18 shows that Jesus Christ is the first in the resurrection of the dead and will have the last word on Judgement Day. Revelation 2:8 also refers to Jesus as the first in the resurrection.

NOTE 14: CHILDREN OF BLESSING

The poem, "Children of blessing," is an important reminder to Christians to remain true to their calling and become real children of their Father who does good to the righteous and the unrighteous, because of his abundant mercy. It also reminds Christians not to repay evil with evil but to bless those who curse them and to pray for them as children of blessing, who will-because of their good deeds- inherit a blessing, that is, eternal life. See the Scriptures below for your edification:

> "Blessed are the peacemakers for they shall be called children of God."
> —Matthew 5:9 NIV

> "Do not repay evil with evil or insult with insult. On the contrary repay evil with blessing, because to this you were called so that you may inherit a blessing."
> —1 Peter 3:9 NIV

> "Bless those who curse you, pray for those who mistreat you."
> —Luke 6:28 NIV

> "But I tell you, love your enemies and pray for those who persecute you, that you may be children of your Father in heaven. He causes his sun to rise on the evil and the good, and sends rain on the righteous and the unrighteous."
> —Matthew 5:44–45 NIV

NOTE 15: CHILDREN OF THE LIGHT

This poem is an exhortation to holiness on the part of Christians-children of the light-who should separate themselves from the sinful world, through love for one another as shown by fellowship and through living righteous lives. Sinners or those living in darkness can be identified through all manner of sin including strife and hatred. In fact, as children of the light, we are urged not to tolerate sin by exposing or rebuking it since light cannot coexist with darkness.

Light and darkness are metaphors for good and bad; righteous and unrighteous, and blameless and sinful; because those who practice sinful acts such as drunkenness and sexual immorality do so at night, while virtuous acts are practised during the day in the full view of everyone. Below, find motivational Scriptures on the subject under review:

> "You are all children of the light and children of the day. We do not belong to the night or the darkness."
> —1 Thessalonians 5:5 NIV

> "If we claim to have fellowship with him and yet walk in the darkness, we lie and do not live out the truth. But if we walk in the light, as he is in the light, we have fellowship with one another, and the blood of Jesus, his Son, purifies us from all sin."
> —1 John 1:6–7 NIV

> "For you were once darkness, but now you are light in the Lord. Live as children of the light (For the fruit of the light consists in all goodness, righteousness and truth) and find out what pleases the Lord. Have nothing to do with the fruitless deeds of darkness, but rather expose them."
> —Ephesians 5:8–11 NIV

NOTE 16: CONTENTMENT

This poem is designed to teach us to be content with what we have. We should ask the Lord Jesus to give us the spirit of contentment and gratitude. See the Scriptures below for further details:

> "I know what it to be in need, and I know what it is to have plenty. I have learnt the secret of being content in any and every situation, whether well fed or hungry, whether living in plenty or in want. I can do this through him who gives me strength."
> —Philippians 4:12–13 NIV

> "For we brought nothing into the world, and we will take nothing out of it. But if we have food and clothing we will be content with that."
> —1 Timothy 6:7–8 NIV

The poem aptly warns us against the danger of the love of money-a form of idolatry-since its unbridled pursuit can lead people into sin. It also shows us that God will always provide for our basic needs, if we maintain our faith. See the Scriptures below for further enlightenment:

> "Keep your lives free from the love of money and be content with what you have because God has said, 'Never will I leave you; never will I forsake you.' "
> —Hebrews 13:5 NIV

> "For the love of money is the root of all evil. Some people, eager for money, have wandered from the faith and pierced themselves with many griefs."
> —1 Timothy 6:10 NIV

NOTE 17: GODLESS CHATTER

This poem warns Christians about the dangers of Godless chatter such as dirty jokes and slanderous talk. The more an individual engages in such behaviour the more they conform to the pattern of the world. Even the sin of adultery begins with the sharing of dirty jokes. Godless chatter, therefore, opens the door to sin. See the Scripture below for further enlightenment:

> "Avoid Godless chatter, because those who indulge in it will become more and more ungodly."
> —2 Timothy 2:16 NIV

NOTE 18: HIS PRECIOUS BLOOD

This poem is designed to show that there is no forgiveness without the shedding of blood, because even in the imperfect old covenant, the blood of goats and calves was sprinkled on people in order to outwardly sanctify them. But when Jesus shed his precious and unblemished blood, he cleansed our consciences from acts that lead to death, thus securing eternal redemption once for all for those who believe in him. See the Scriptures below for your encouragement:

> "But when Christ came as high priest of the good things that are now already here, he went through the perfect tabernacle that is not made with human hands, that is to say, is not a part of this creation. He did not enter by means of the blood of goats and calves; but he entered the Most Holy place once for all by his own blood, thus obtaining eternal redemption."
> —Hebrews 9:11–12 NIV

> "In fact, the law requires that nearly everything be cleansed with blood and without the shedding of blood there is no forgiveness."
> —Hebrews 9:22 NIV

NOTE 19: REAL FAITH

The poem, "Real faith," shows us that if faith is not accompanied by appropriate action, it is ineffective and sterile, and cannot achieve the required results. See the Scripture below on this subject:

> "In the same way, faith by itself, if not accompanied by action, is dead."
> —James 2:17 NIV

The significance of acting out one's faith is demonstrated by Abraham, who when called to go to the Promised Land, actually set out on the journey, even though he did not know where he was going because he believed that he who had called him was faithful and would guide his steps. The result of Abraham's obedience is that the Israelites eventually inherited the Promised Land. See the Scripture below for further encouragement:

> "By faith Abraham when called to go to a place he would receive as an inheritance, obeyed and went, even though he did not know where he was going."
> —Hebrews 11:8 NIV

Whatever you are believing for, step out in faith with the accompanying action. What is it that God has promised you? If it's a job, step out in faith and send out the applications. If it's a baby, step out in faith and buy baby clothes. If it's a house, step out in faith and have the plan designed.

NOTE 20: PUT YOUR TRUST IN GOD

This poem is a reminder to Christians not to rely too much on their capabilities, but to always commit their plans and problems to God who is both omnipotent and indomitable. See the following Scriptures for further encouragement:

> "Some trust in chariots and some in horses, but we trust in the name of the LORD our God."
> —Psalm 20:7 NIV

> "I am the LORD, the God of all mankind. Is anything too hard for me?"
> —Jeremiah 32:27 NIV

NOTE 21: RECEIVING FROM GOD

While the poem looks at only two keys to receiving from God: asking and asking with the right motives; two more: faith and righteousness, can also be added. See the Scriptures below for your instruction:

> "You do not have because you do not ask God."
> —James 4:2c NIV

> "But when you ask, you must believe and not doubt because the one who doubts is like a wave of the sea, blown and tossed by the wind. That person should not expect to receive anything from the Lord."
> —James 1:6–7 NIV

> "When you ask you do not receive because you ask with wrong motives, that you may spend what you get on your pleasures."
> —James 4:3 NIV

> "Dear friends, if our hearts do not condemn us, we have confidence before God and receive from him anything we ask, because we keep his commands and do what pleases him."
> —1 John 3:21–22 NIV

NOTE 22: RECONCILIATION

The poem on reconciliation enjoins us to be Christ's ambassadors since he was the mediator of God's reconciliation with sinful humanity. As Christians, we are called upon to be the mediators of reconciliation with the enemies of God. And as co-workers with Christ, we should never shy away from witnessing about God's grace; even in the face of intense persecution. Below, see the relevant Scriptures for further details:

> "Once you were alienated from God and were enemies in your minds because of your evil behaviour. But now he has reconciled you by Christ's physical body through death to present you holy in his sight, without blemish and free from accusation."
> —Colossians 1:21–22 NIV

> "All this is from God who reconciled us to himself through Christ and gave us the ministry of reconciliation: that God was

reconciling the world to himself in Christ, not counting people's sins against them. And he has committed to us the message of reconciliation."
—2 Corinthians 5:18–19 NIV

NOTE 23: REFINING FURNACE OF SUFFERING

This poem shows us that God sometimes allows suffering in our lives as a means for exercising our faith muscle, and to refining our character, just as gold passes through fire for its refinement. See the Scripture below for further details:

"Not only so, but we glory in our sufferings, because we know that suffering produces perseverance, perseverance character and character hope."
—Romans 5:3–4 NIV

NOTE 24: REWARD FOR GENEROSITY

This poem is an exhortation to the virtue of generosity, as it shows that the more we give is the more we receive. In fact the poem shows that God's provision will go out to all those who are of a generous disposition. See the encouraging Scriptures below:

"Give and it will be given to you. A good measure, pressed down, shaken together and running over will be poured into your lap. For with the measure you use, it will be measured to you."
—Luke 6:38 NIV

"Remember this: Whoever sows sparingly will also reap sparingly, and whoever sows generously will also reap generously."
—2 Corinthians 9:6 NIV

"And my God will meet all your needs according to the riches of his glory in Christ Jesus."
—Philippians 4:19 NIV

Notes

NOTE 25: THE DILIGENT WORKER

This poem seeks to promote the virtue of diligence among Christian workers, who should serve as though they were serving Jesus, their ultimate "rewarder." See the Scriptures below for your edification:

> "Whatever you do, work at it with all your heart, as working for the Lord, not for human masters, since you know that you will receive an inheritance from the Lord as a reward. It is the Lord Christ you are serving."
> —Colossians 3:23–24 NIV

> "Look, I am coming soon! My reward is with me, and I will give to each person according to what they have done."
> —Revelation 22:12 NIV

NOTE 26: THE FAITHFUL WITNESS

This poem shows that Jesus Christ empathizes with us and is therefore a merciful and faithful witness, who is able to intercede for our sins before the Father since he experienced all manner of trial and temptation during his time on earth. See the Scripture cited below for further details:

> "For this reason he had to be made like them, fully human in every way, in order that he might become a merciful and faithful high priest in service to God, and that he might make atonement for the sins of the people. Because he himself suffered when he was tempted, he is able to help those who are being temped."
> —Hebrews 2:17–18 NIV

NOTE 27: TRUE PROPHECY

This poem shows that any prophecy coming from the Lord will come to pass as revealed by the Scripture cited below:

> "If what a prophet proclaims in the name of the LORD does not take place or come true, that is a message the LORD has not spoken. That prophet has spoken presumptuously, so do not be alarmed."
> —Deuteronomy 18:22 NIV

Again, any message that comes from the Lord must be in line with sound doctrine. This is the reason why the church is admonished to test all prophecies:

> "Do not treat prophecies with contempt but test them all; hold onto what is good, reject every kind of evil."
> —1 Thessalonians 5:20–22 NIV

NOTE 28: WALKING BY THE SPIRIT

The poem, "Walking by the Spirit," is an exhortation to live a holy life, separated from those who live to please the flesh. See the Scripture below for your edification:

> "So I say, walk by the Spirit, and you will not gratify the desires of the flesh. For the flesh desires what is contrary to the Spirit and the Spirit what is contrary to the flesh."
> —Galatians 5:16–17a NIV

Walking by the Spirit means not yielding to the desires of the flesh such as those cited below:

> "The acts of the flesh are obvious: sexual immorality, impurity and debauchery; idolatry and witchcraft; hatred, discord, jealousy, fits of rage, selfish ambition, dissensions, factions and envy; drunkenness, orgies and the like."
> **—Galatians 5:19–21a NIV**

But those who walk by the Spirit display a different disposition. See the Scripture below for further details:

> "But the fruit of the Spirit is love, joy, peace, forbearance, kindness, boldness, faithfulness, gentleness and self-control. Against such things there is no law."
> —Galatians 5:22–23 NIV

Those who walk by the Spirit inherit eternal life because they have crucified the flesh and its desires, while those who live by the flesh will be consigned to eternal anguish in hell.

NOTE 29: DISCIPLINE

This poem shows us that God sometimes draws us to himself through unexplained failure and suffering Therefore, in the face of failure and lack of progress, we are called upon to self-introspect and correct our ways. See some of the Scriptures on discipline below:

> "Those whom I love I rebuke and discipline."
> —Revelation 3:19a NIV

> "Endure hardship as discipline; God is treating you as his children. For what children are not disciplined-and everyone undergoes discipline-then you are not legitimate, not true sons and daughters at all."
> —Hebrews 12:7 NIV

> "But God disciplines us for our good, in order that we may share in his holiness. No discipline seems pleasant at the time, but painful. Later on, however, it produces a harvest of righteousness and peace for those who have been trained by it."
> —Hebrews 12:10b–11 NIV

NOTE 30: HEZEKIAH

The poem on Hezekiah underlines the significance of righteousness as a key to answered prayer. The Scripture below attests to Hezekiah's righteousness:

> "He did what was right in the eyes of the LORD, just as his father David had done . . . Hezekiah trusted in the LORD, the God of Israel. There was no one like him among all the kings of Judah either before him or after him. He held fast to the LORD and did not stop following him: he kept the commands God had given Moses."
> —2 Kings 18:3; 5–6 NIV

The effectiveness of the prayer of a righteous man can be vividly illustrated by Elijah, who prayed that it would not rain and it never did for three and a half years. But when he also prayed that it rained again, it also did.

So when Hezekiah-a righteous man-prayed that God might heal him from a deadly disease, he was healed and also had fifteen more years added to his life. See the Scripture below for your encouragement:

> "Hezekiah turned his face to the wall and prayed to the LORD, "Remember LORD, how I have walked before you faithfully and with wholehearted devotion and have done what is good in your eyes." And Hezekiah wept bitterly."
> —2 Kings 20:2–3 NIV

The lesson to be learnt from the story of Hezekiah is that righteousness can act as a key to answered prayer. Therefore, Hezekiah's poem is urging believers to examine their hearts for any sin that may be acting as a barrier to God's answer for their petitions, as God is faithful and will always forgive those who earnestly seek his righteousness. Believers should always pray for the filling of the Holy Spirit in order that they may be sanctified.

NOTE 31: HIGHER GLORY

This poem is a call to believers to persevere and remain hopeful for the higher glory of eternal bliss, knowing well that our present sufferings are only temporary and cannot be compared to the joy that awaits us. See the Scripture below for your encouragement:

> "I consider that our present sufferings are not worth comparing with the glory that will be revealed in us."
> —Romans 8:18 NIV

Indeed the word of God values perseverance as a virtue and aptly calls on believers not to be distracted by anything from attaining the higher glory of eternity:

> "Who shall separate us from the love of Christ? Shall trouble or hardship or persecution or famine or nakedness or danger or sword?"
> —Romans 8:35 NIV

Sometimes God uses the lowly state of suffering to produce the higher states of perseverance and the character of faith, resulting in the hope of eternal glory. See the Scripture cited below for more details:

> "No only so, but we glory in our sufferings, because we know that suffering produces perseverance, perseverance character and character hope."
> —Romans 5:3–4 NIV

God can also allow the lowly state of suffering to produce for us the higher state of humility. See Paul's confession cited below:

> "Therefore, in order to keep me from being conceited, I was given a thorn in my flesh, a messenger of Satan, to torment me."
> —2 Corinthians 12:7b NIV

NOTE 32: OMNIPOTENT GOD

The omnipotent God refers collectively to all the divine personalities comprising the Holy Trinity. Below, are scriptural faith building affirmations on God's omnipotence to unlock your total faith and dependence on him:

> "I am the LORD, the God of all mankind. Is anything too hard for me?"
> —Jeremiah 32:27 NIV

> "What he opens no one can shut and what he shuts no one can open."
> —Revelation 3:7c NIV

> "Yes, and from ancient days I am he. No one can deliver out of my hand. When I act, who can reverse it?"
> —Isaiah 43:13 NIV

> "There is no wisdom, no insight, no plan that can succeed against the LORD."
> —Proverbs 21:30 NIV

Christians should take comfort in the knowledge that if we depend on God's protection, he will not let our enemies triumph over us, because:

> "If God is for us, who can be against us?"
> —Romans 6:36 NIV

Please note that our enemies can be testing, want, sickness, demonic oppression, and so forth.

NOTE 33: OMNISCIENT GOD

This poem is designed to celebrate God's omniscience and to call readers to holiness and righteousness, for no one is able to hide their sins from God. See the following Scriptures for further details:

> "I make known the end from the beginning, from ancient times, what is still to come."
> —Isaiah 46:10a NIV

> "Nothing in all creation is hidden from God's sight. Everything is uncovered and laid bare before the eyes of him to whom we must give account."
> —Hebrews 4:13 NIV

> "Woe to those who go to great depths to hide their plans from the LORD, who do their work in darkness and think, "Who sees us? Who will know?" "
> —Isaiah 29:15 NIV

To demonstrate God's omniscience, Jesus had this to say regarding judgement:

> "There is nothing concealed that will not be disclosed, or hidden that will not be made known. What you have said in the dark will be heard in broad daylight, and what you have whispered in the ear in the inner rooms will be proclaimed from the roofs."
> —Luke 12:2–3 NIV

www.ingramcontent.com/pod-product-compliance
Lightning Source LLC
Chambersburg PA
CBHW071744040426
42446CB00012B/2463